SHAPES to CUT

Food

Illustrated by Gary Mohrman

Teaching & Learning Company

1204 Buchanan St., P.O. Box 10
Carthage, IL 62321-0010

Table of Contents

Apple	5	Hamburger	19
Bacon	6	Hot Dog	20
Banana	7	Ice Cream Cone	21
Bowl of Cereal	8	Lemon	22
Cake	9	Lettuce	23
Carrot	10	Orange	24
Cheese	11	Peach	25
Chicken Leg	12	Pear	26
Cookie	13	Pie	27
Cupcake	14	Pineapple	28
Ear of Corn	15	Pizza	29
Eggplant	16	Sandwich	30
Fried Egg	17	Tomato	31
Grapes	18	Watermelon	32

Cover by Gary Mohrman

Copyright © 1998, Teaching & Learning Company

ISBN No. 1-57310-133-8

Printing No. 9876543

Teaching & Learning Company
1204 Buchanan St., P.O. Box 10
Carthage, IL 62321-0010

The purchase of this book entitles teachers to make copies for use in their individual classrooms only. This book, or any part of it, may not be reproduced in any form for any other purposes without prior written permission from the Teaching & Learning Company. It is strictly prohibited to reproduce any part of this book for an entire school or school district, or for commercial resale.

All rights reserved. Printed in the United States of America.

How to Use This Book

The patterns in this book provide simple shapes with round corners, thick lines, gentle angles and useful images for your children's first cutting experiences. Use the shapes individually to enhance a learning center or unit or use them in combination to create lively learning experiences.

It is usually easier if the children color the picture first and then cut it out. Some interesting effects can be achieved by having the children color white paper with markers (crayons and watercolors not recommended) and then copying the image onto the colored paper. If you do not want the children to color the picture, then you might copy it onto colored paper.

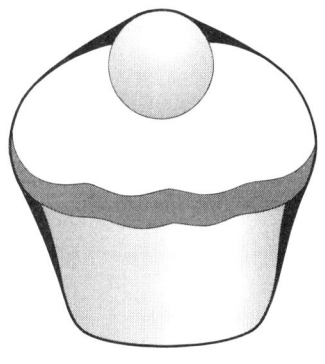

color shape    **marker paper** 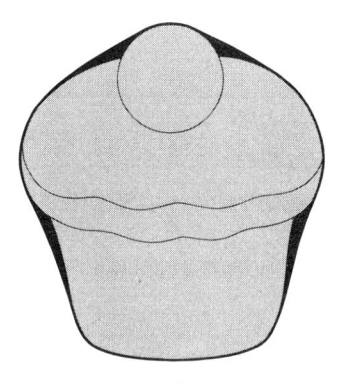   **colored paper**

Other ideas include:
- tracing the picture onto thin interfacing (found in fabric stores) and coloring with marker. These make wonderful flannel board items.
- cutting the pattern out of tagboard or plastic (large ice cream container lids work well, check your school cafeteria) and using as a stencil.
- cutting the pattern out of a sponge and using for sponge painting.

Some things you can make with these patterns:

Puffy Stuff

Make fronts and backs. Before gluing shut, fill with a small amount of cotton batting or paper towel.

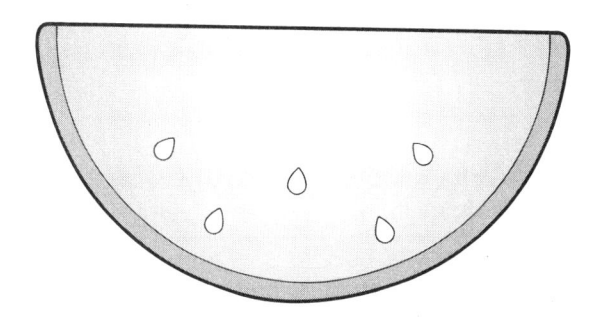

Flash Cards

Write beginning sounds or other facts on the shapes, use for review.

Mobiles

Make fronts and backs and hang from a coat hanger with string or yarn.

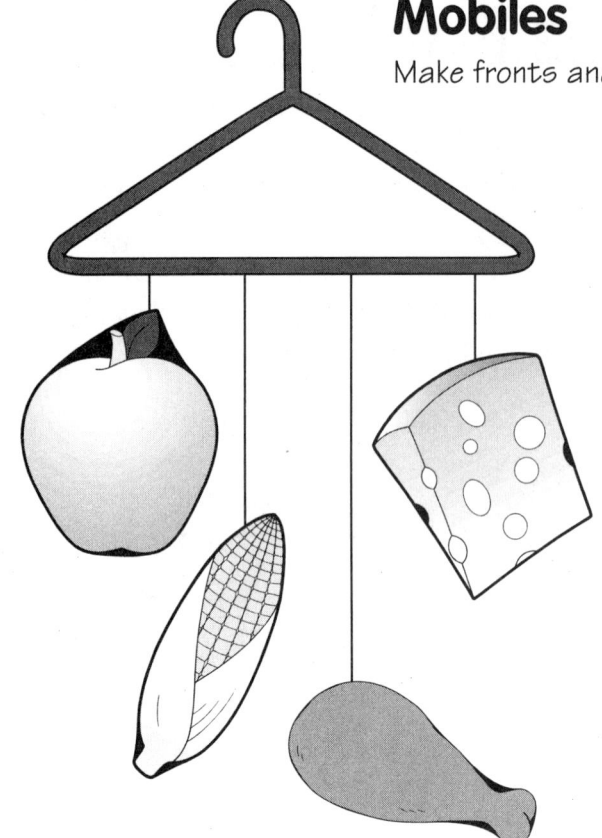

Stick Puppets

Attach a craft stick to the back and use to tell a story.

Shape Books

Some more things you can make with these patterns:

- bulletin board displays, door decorations, window decals
- name tags or place cards
- stationery
- portfolio covers or report covers
- flannel board pieces (cut from flannel or interfacing)
- gift wrap (cut from sponge and dip in tempera paint for sponge painting)
- stand-up figures (Make a front and back and glue together. Stand up with a small amount of clay.)
- sorting materials (Copy onto colored paper. Make sure you have at least two of the items in the same color. Cut out. Have children sort by color, shape, etc.)

You'll find many creative uses for the patterns in this book, and your young children will love having a collection of shapes to cut!

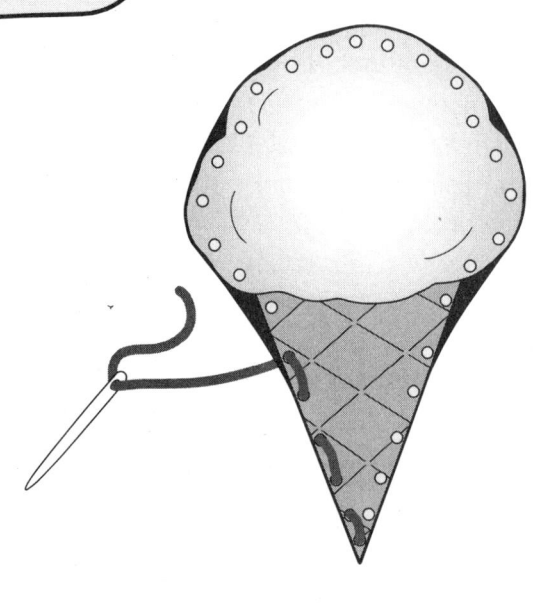

Lacing Items

Cut pattern from felt, glue two or three thicknesses together for strength. Use a hole punch to make holes around the edges about 1" (2.5 cm) apart. Supply blunt plastic needle and length of yarn.

TLC10133 Copyright © Teaching & Learning Company, Carthage, IL 62321-0010

Apple

Bacon

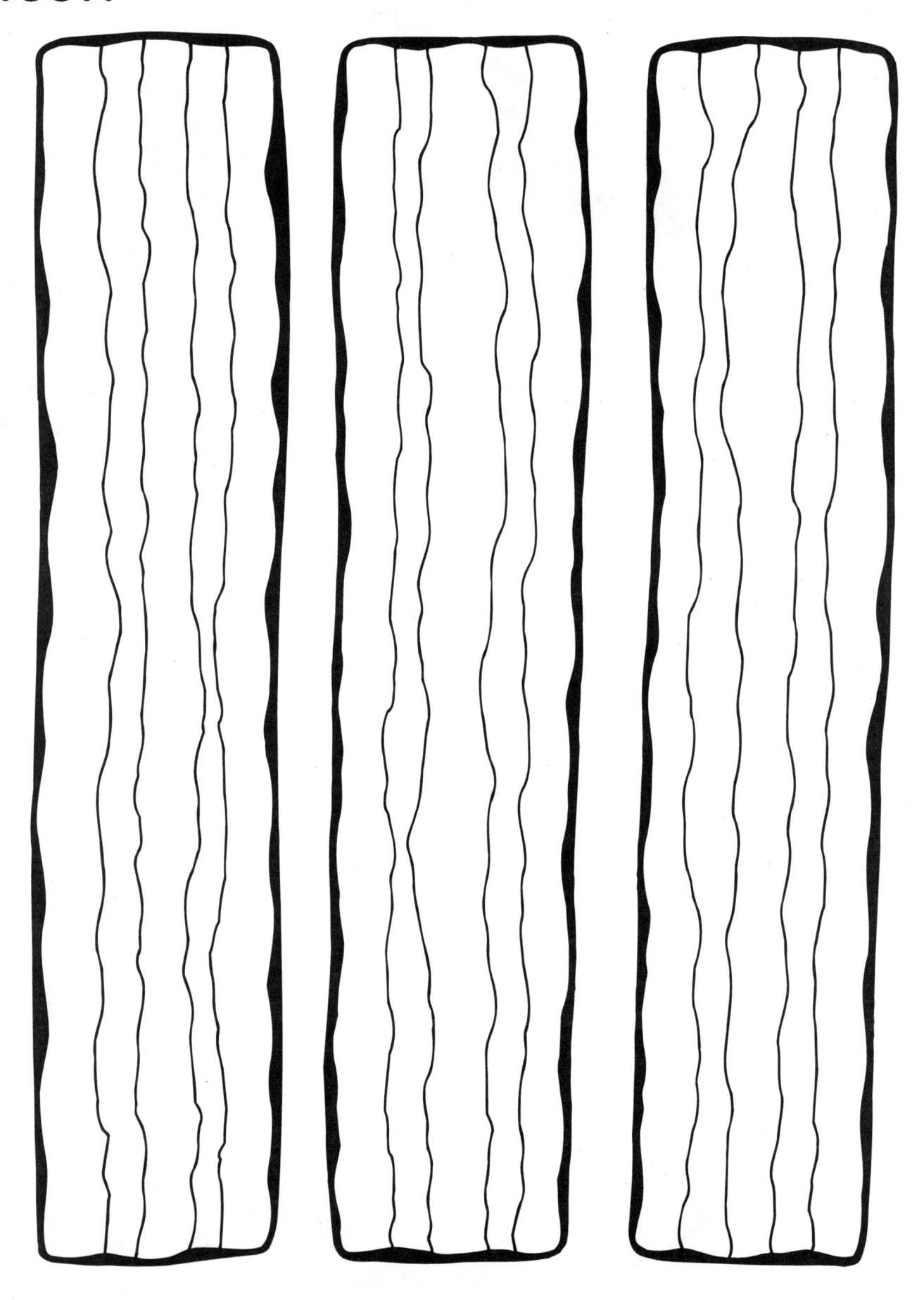

Banana

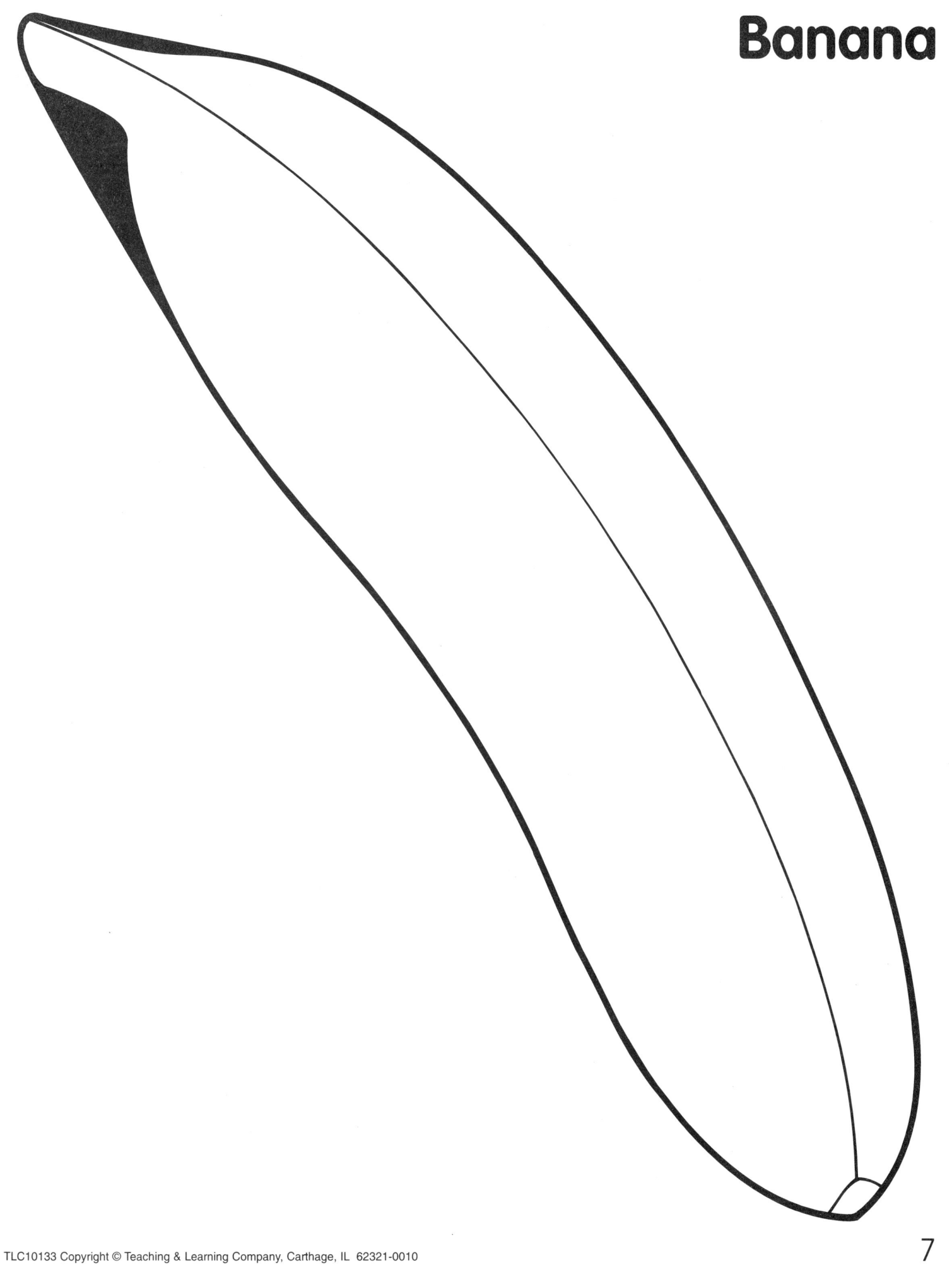

Bowl of Cereal

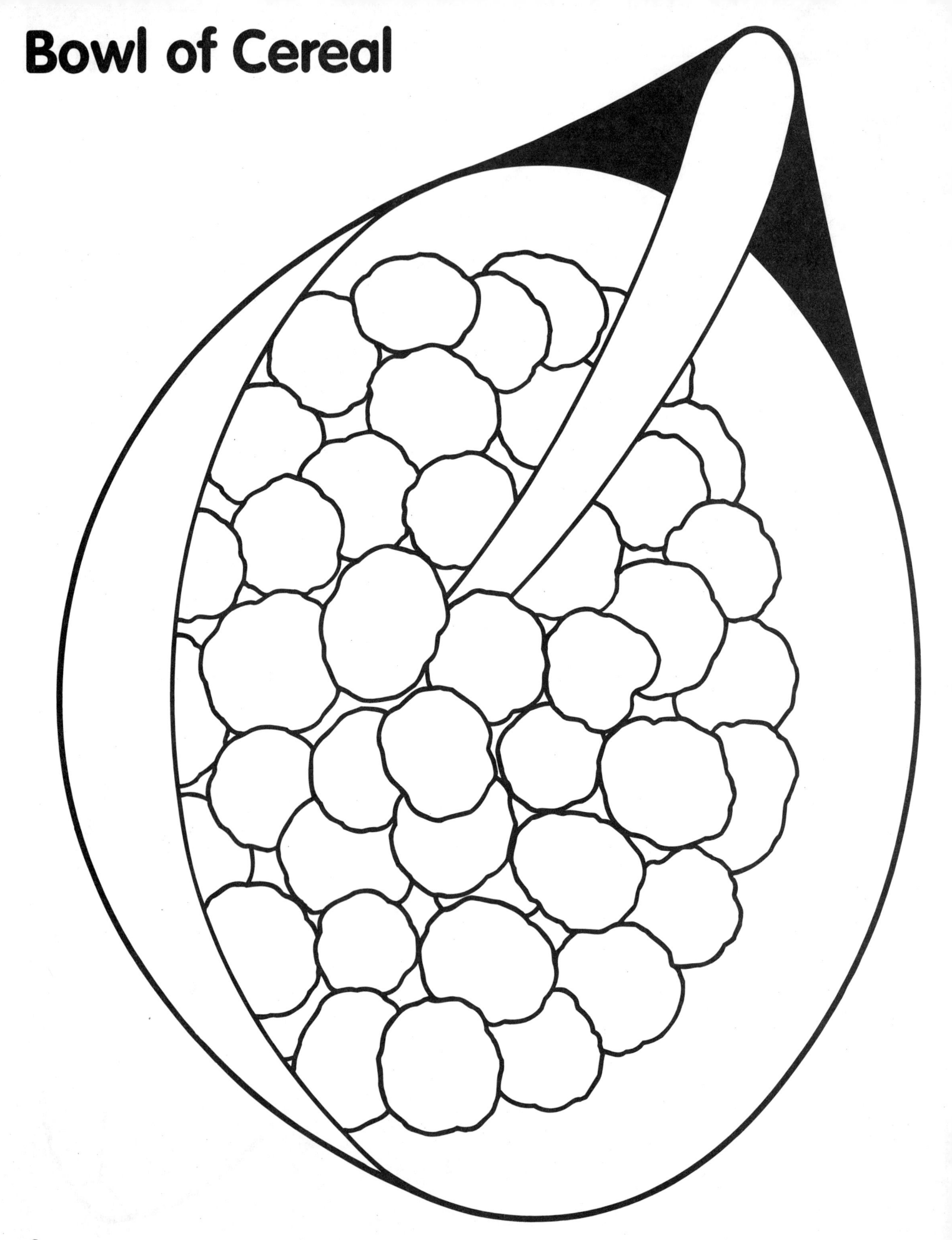

Cake

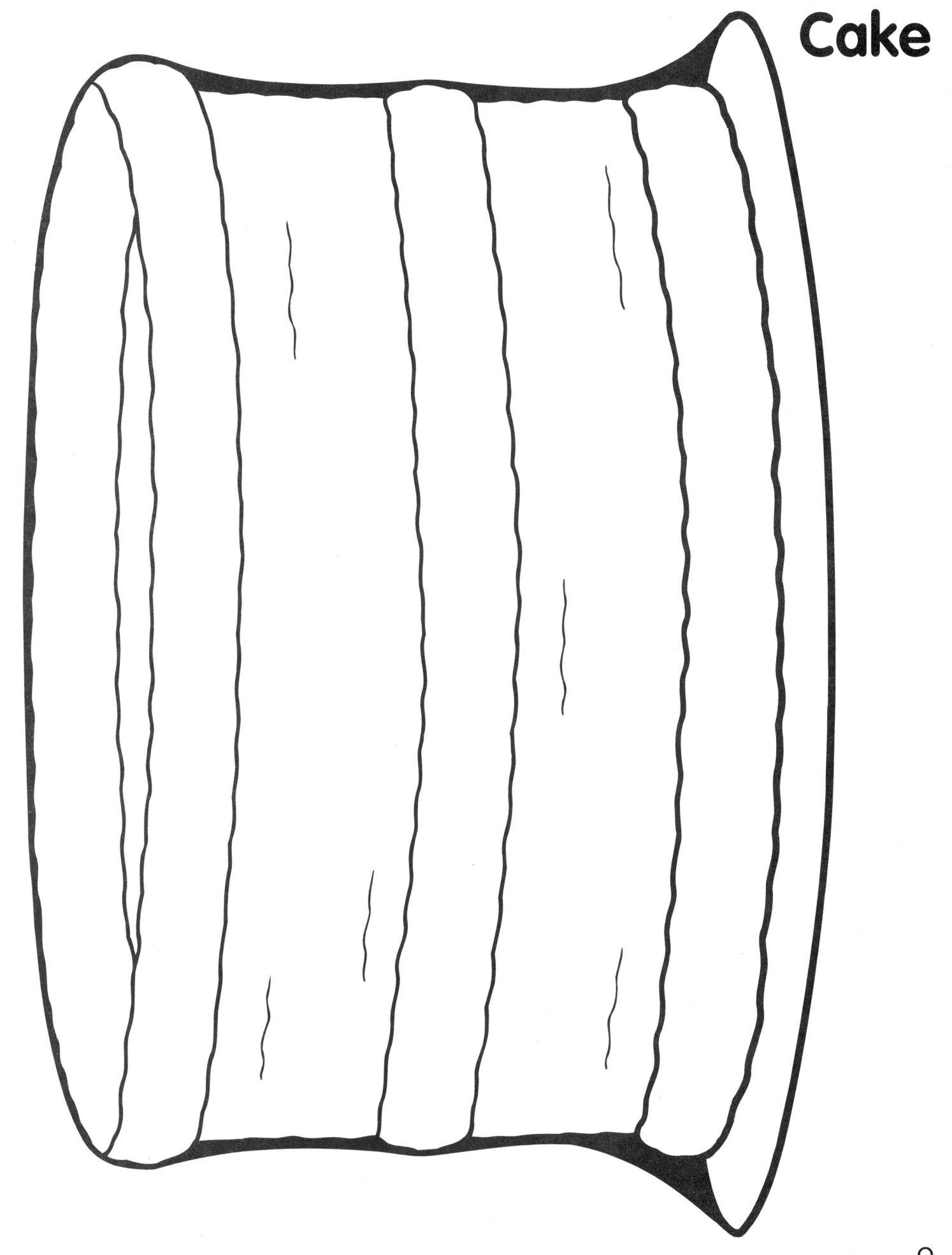

Carrot

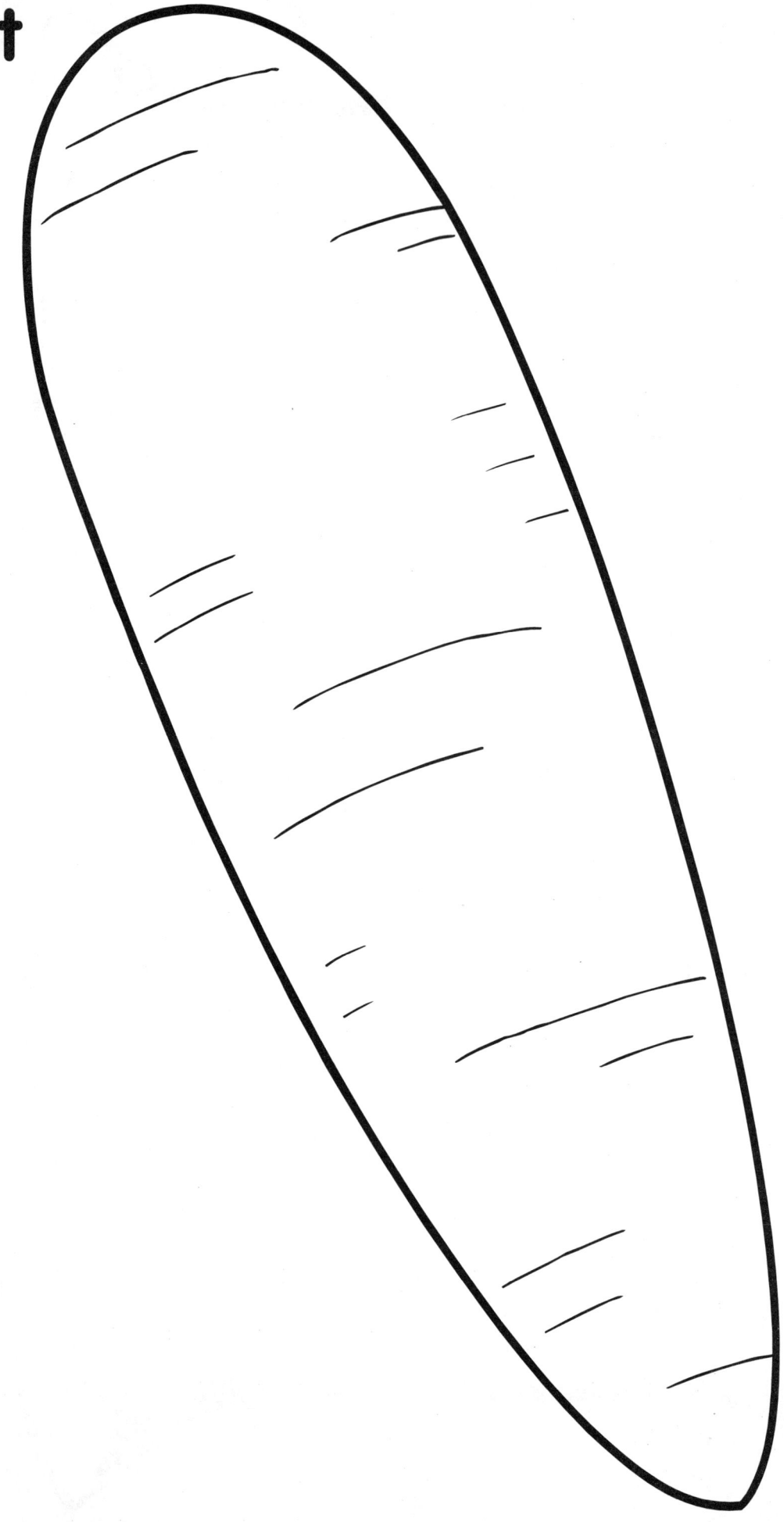

Cheese

Chicken Leg

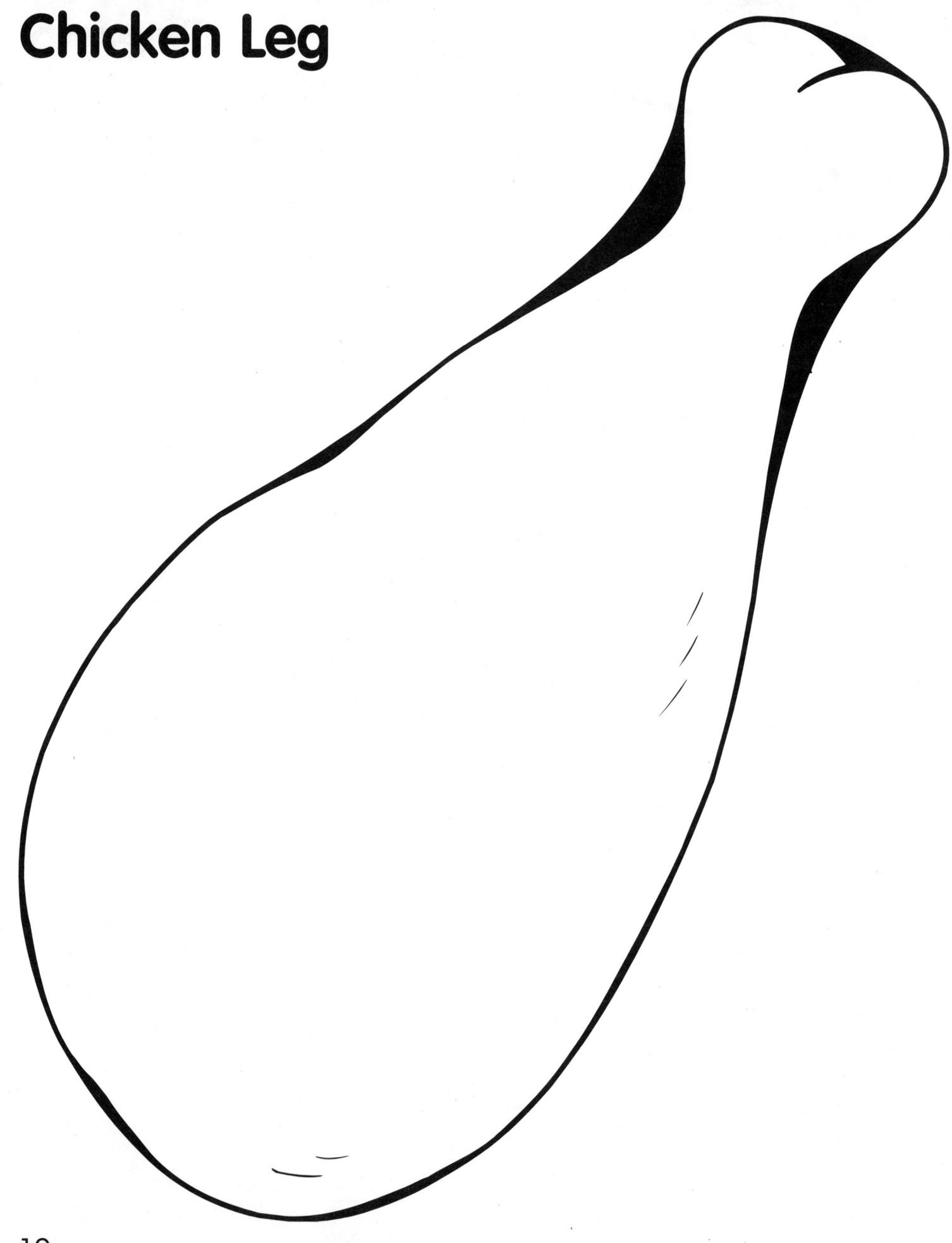

Cookie

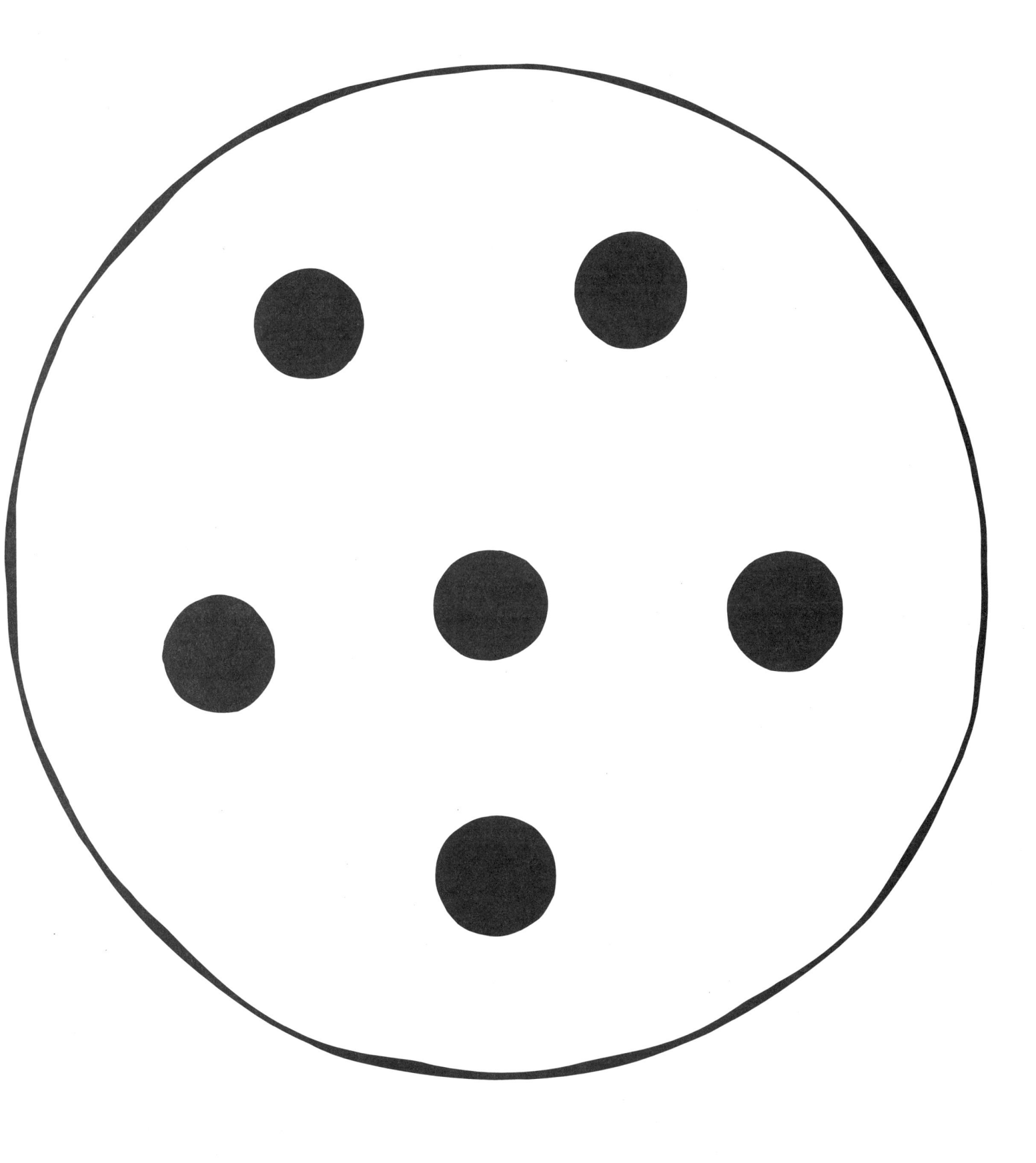

Cupcake

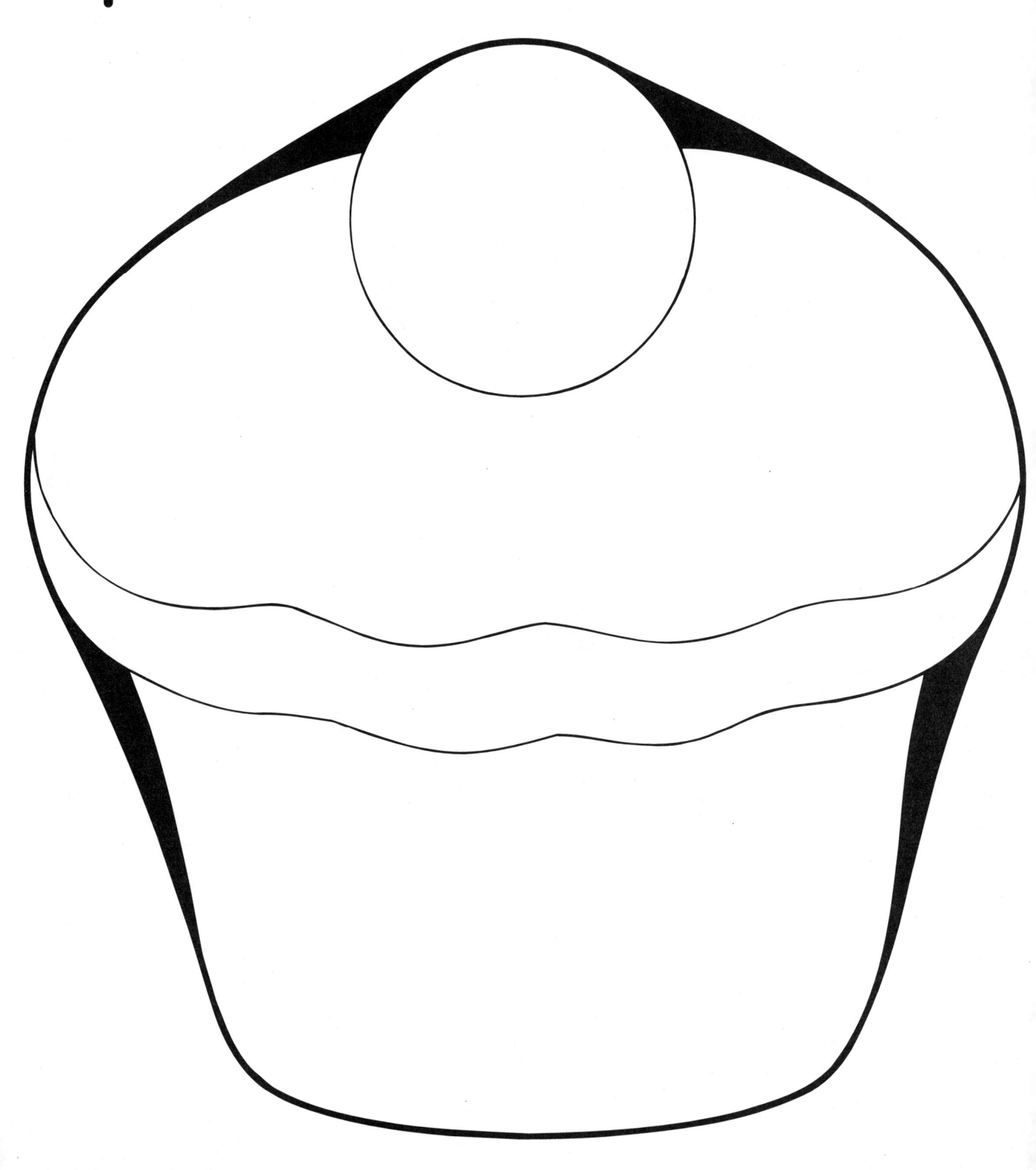

Ear of Corn

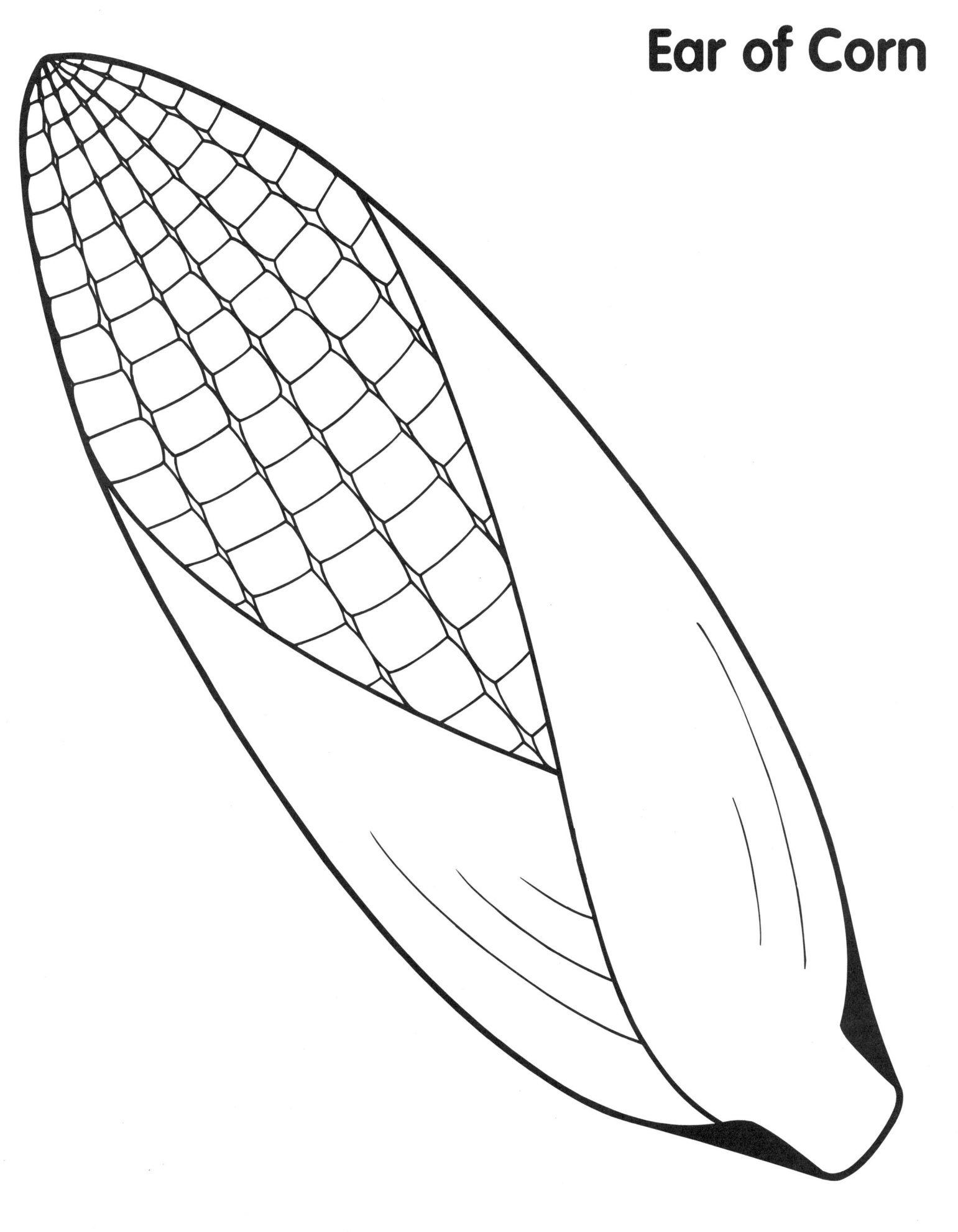

Eggplant

Fried Egg

Grapes

Hamburger

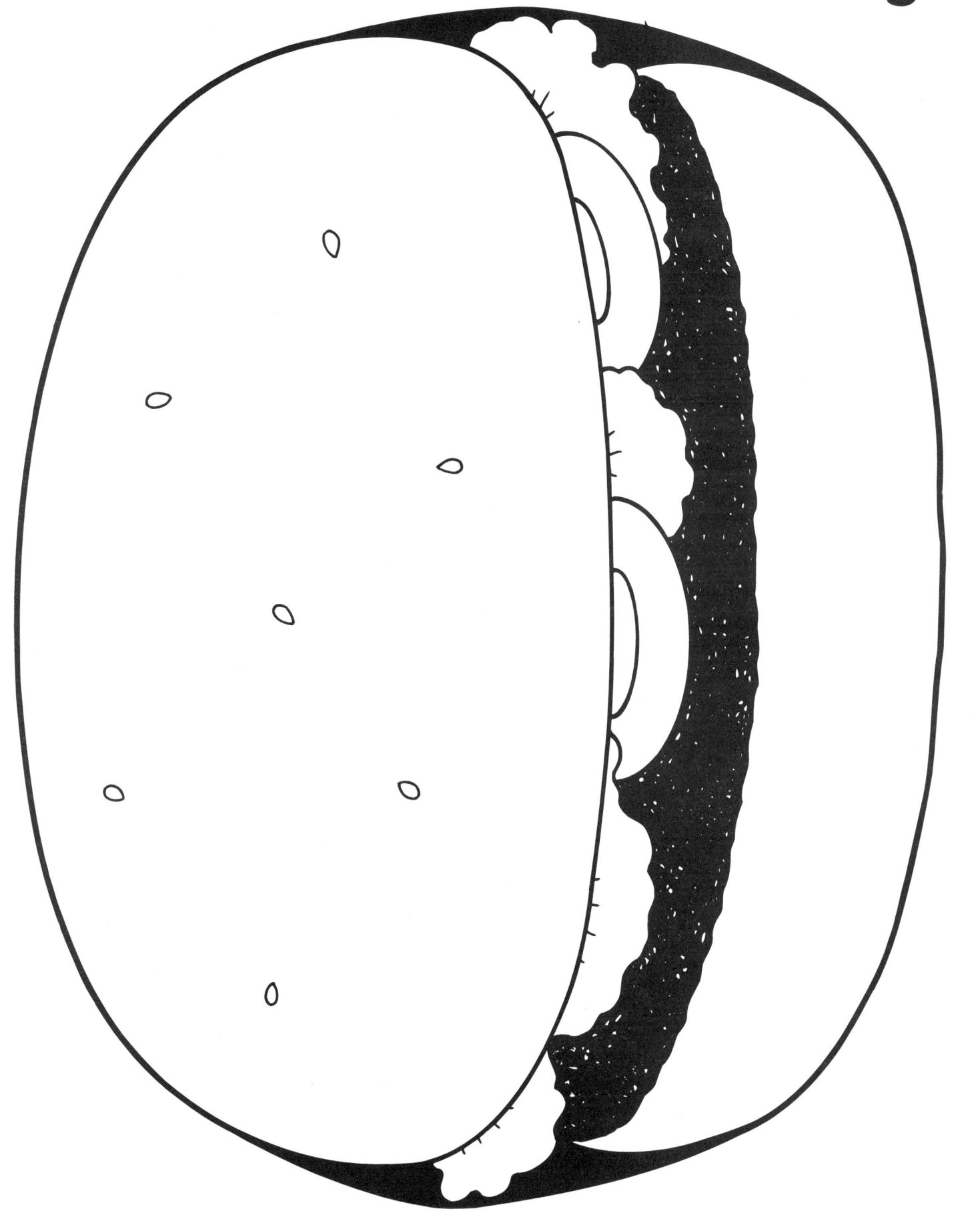

Hot Dog

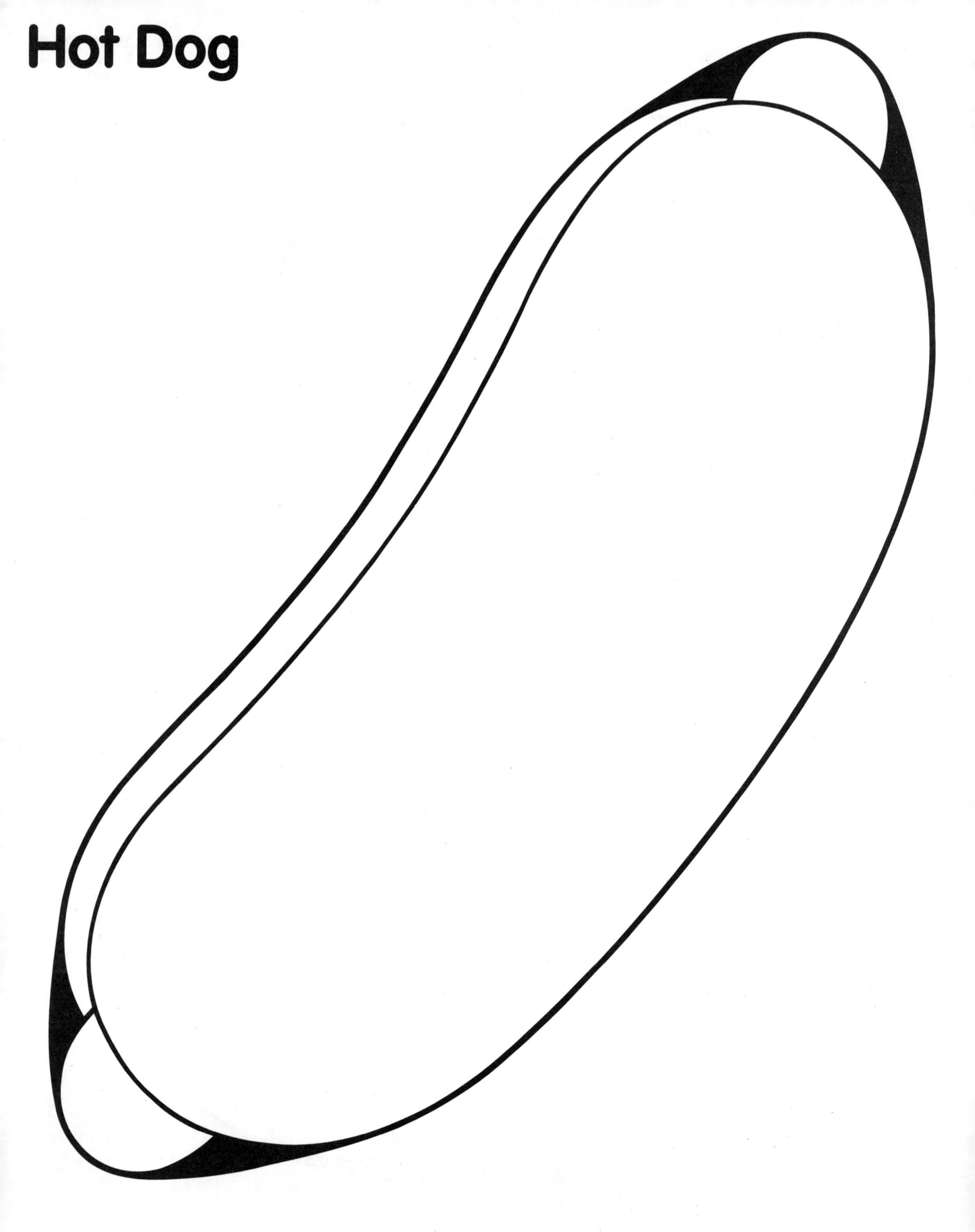

Ice Cream Cone

Lemon

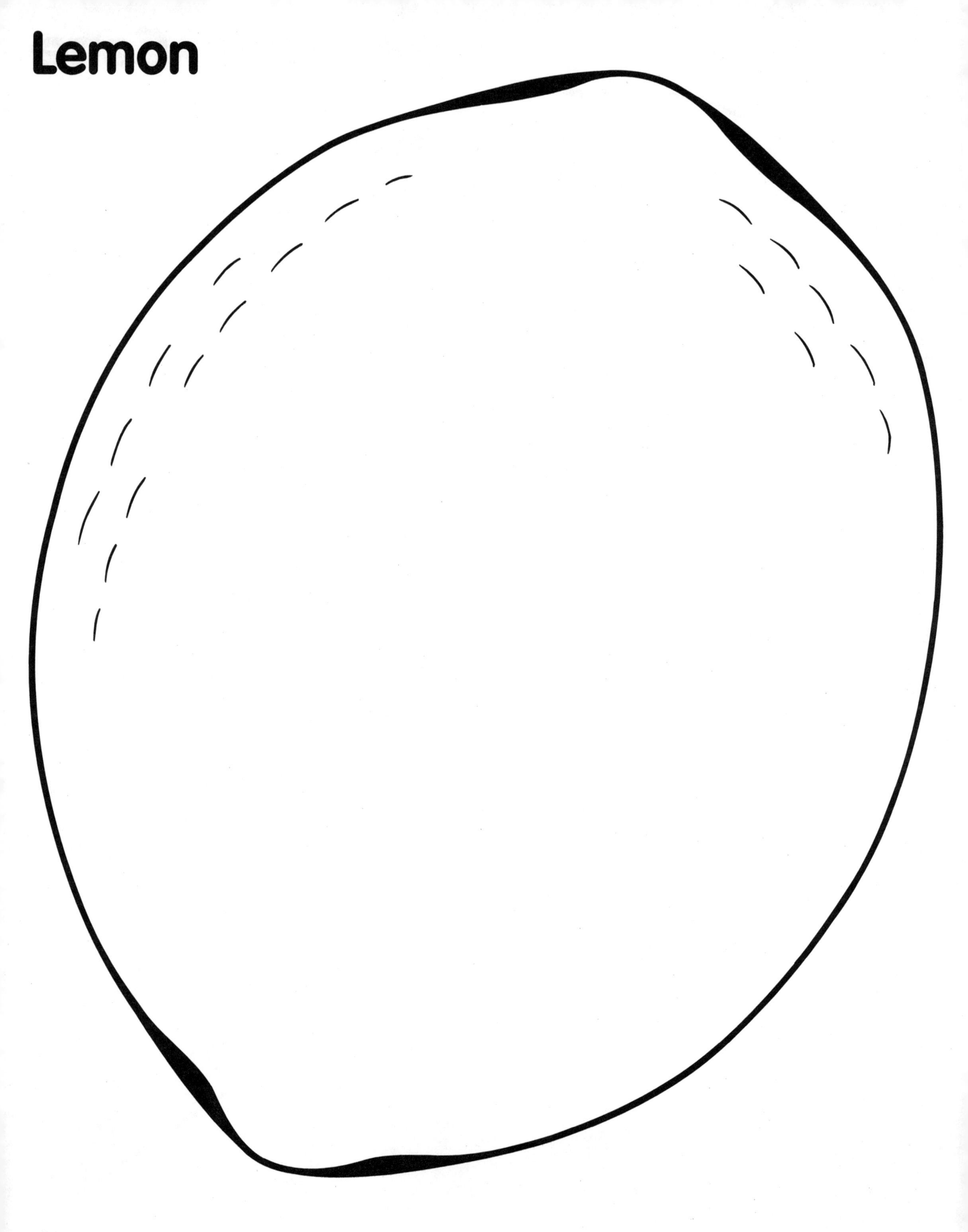

Lettuce

Orange

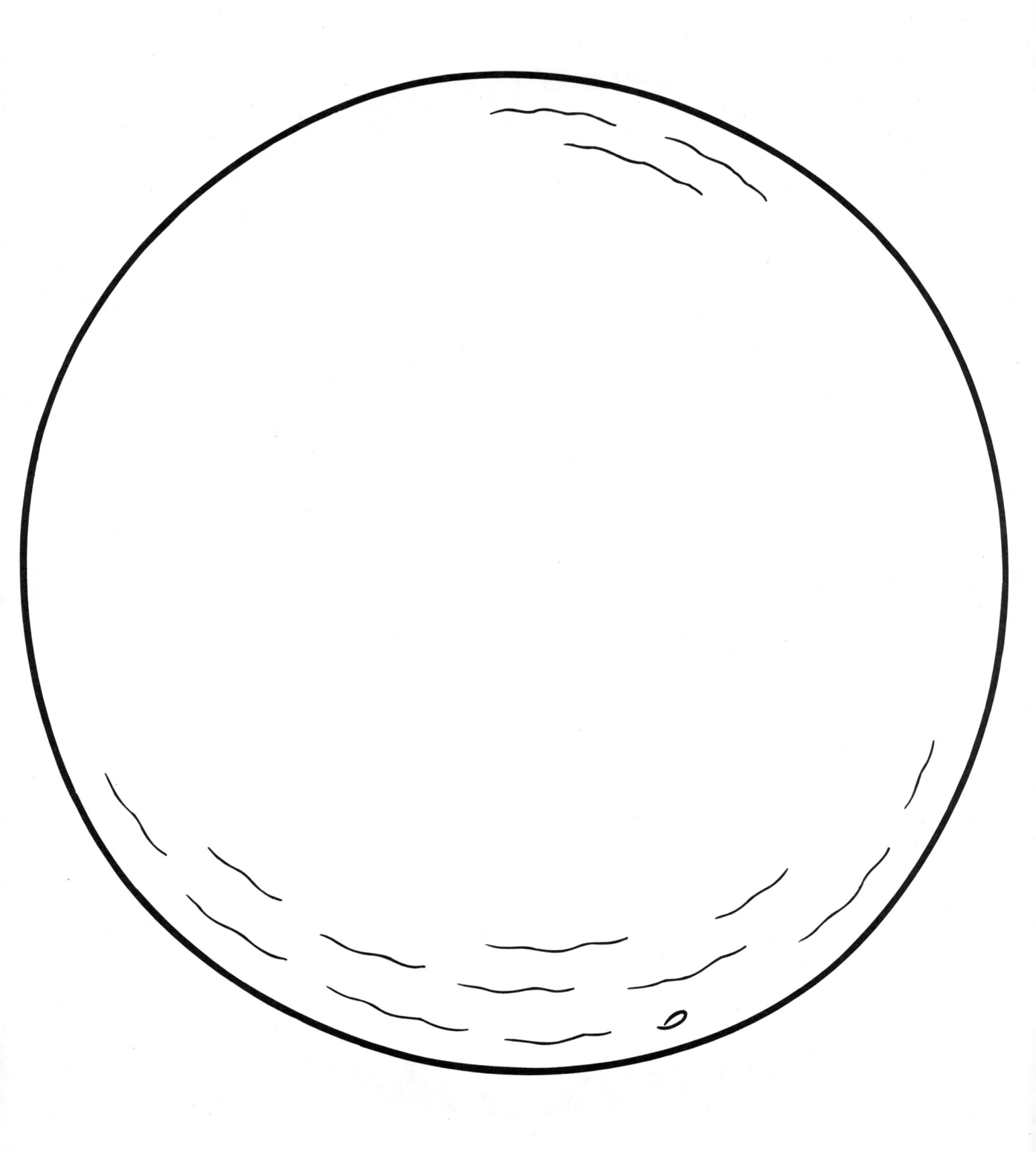

Peach

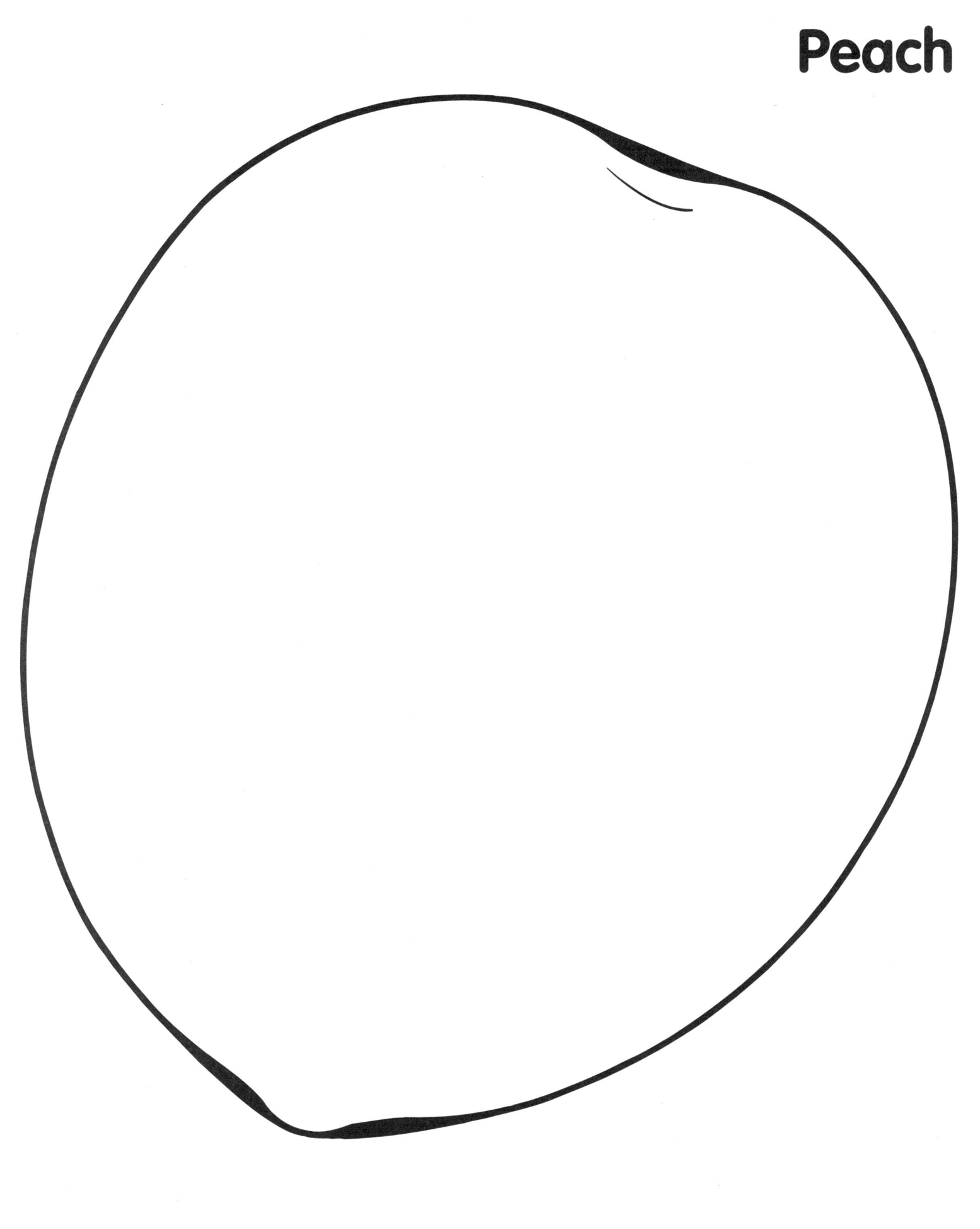

Pear

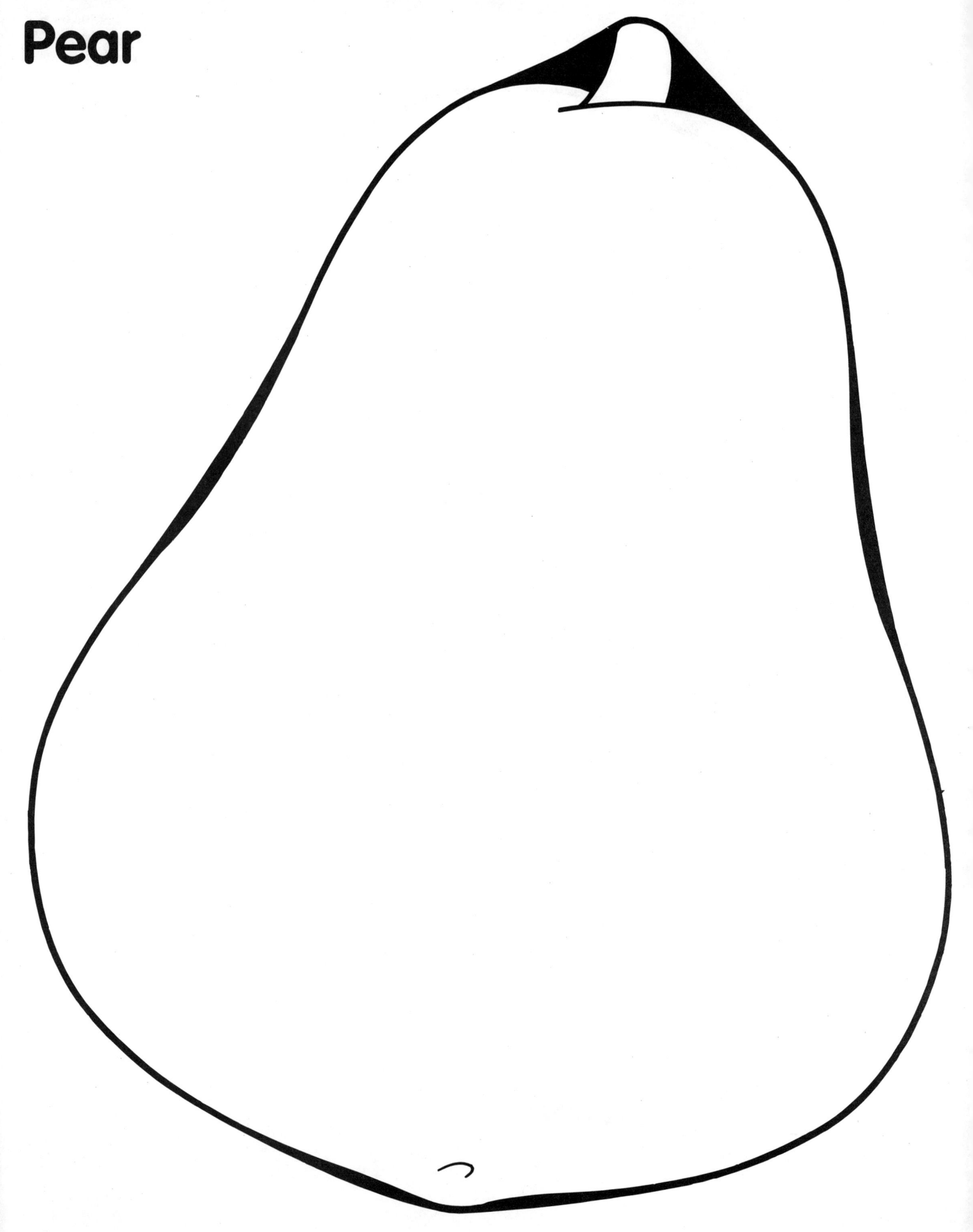

Pie

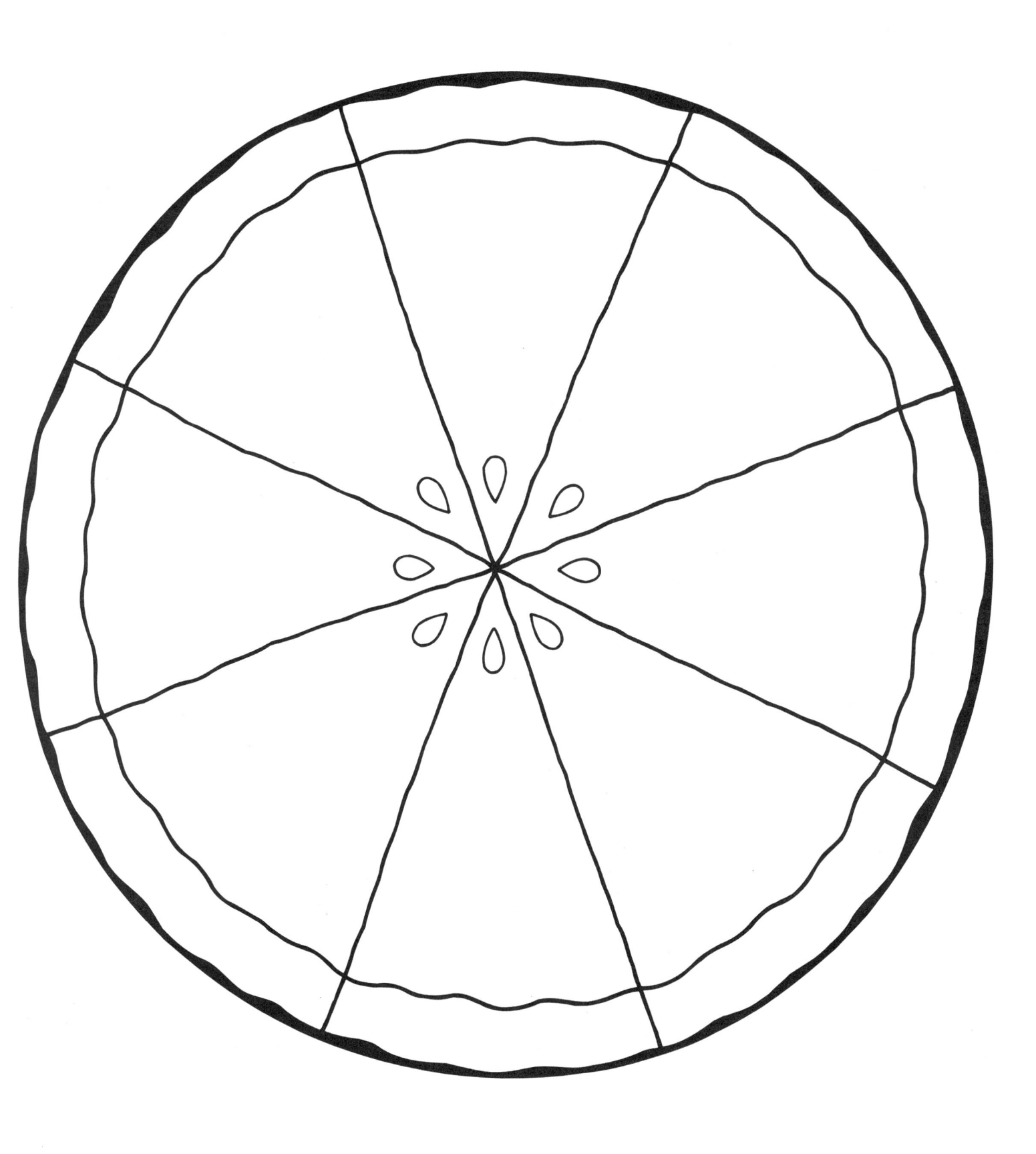

27

Pineapple

Pizza

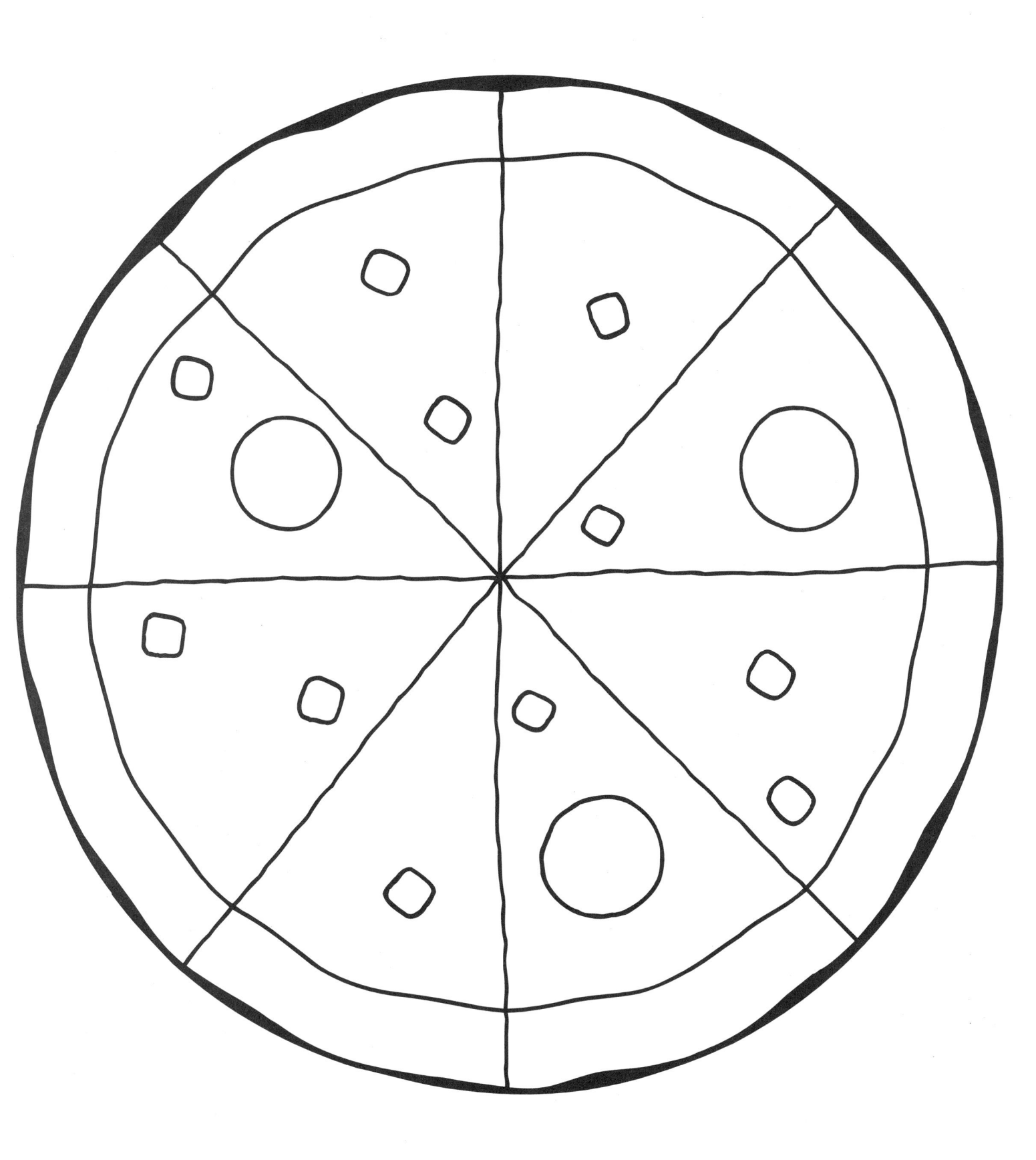

29

Sandwich

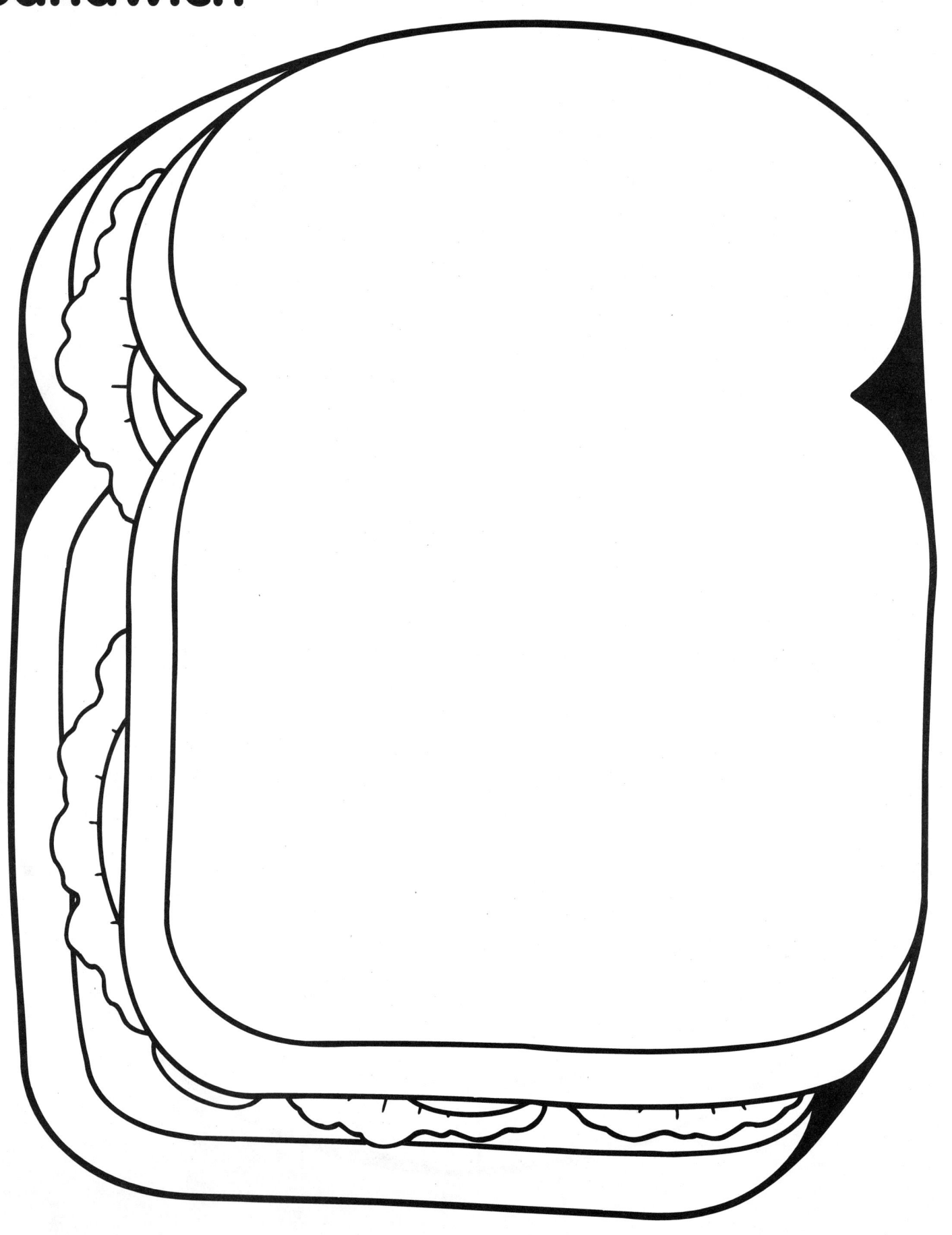

Tomato

Watermelon

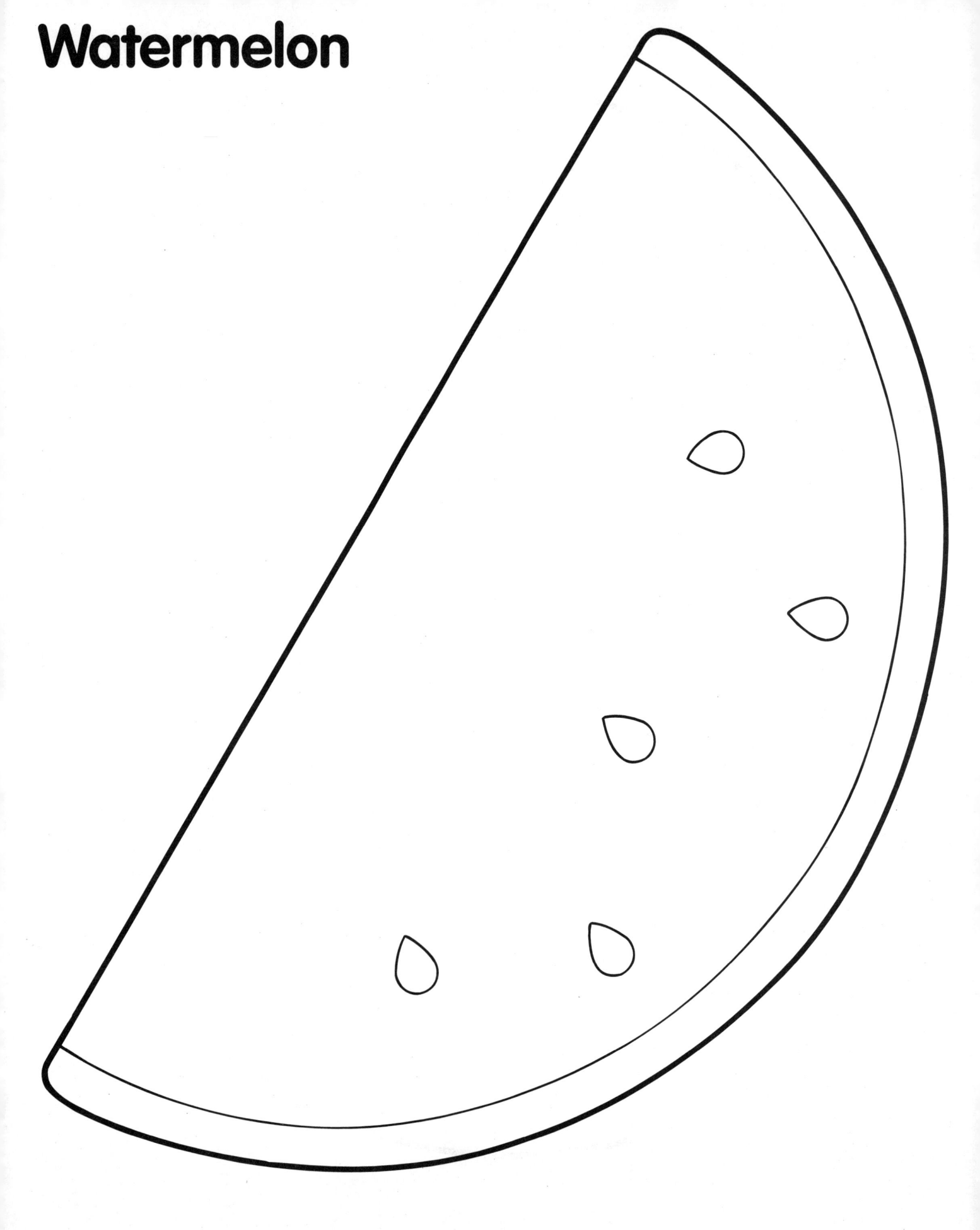